"Patrick Errington's poems are conceived in attention, crafted in grace, and finished in wisdom. 'They told me as a child to be exact with pain,' Errington writes, and his poems are true to his credo, leaping wildly through the mysteries of mourning while extending to us the compassionate hand of form. Here is a poet who knows that form and freedom can be one, that sorrow can have an ecstasy within it, that hope might just be 'loss finding what form it can keep.' Here, in poem after poem, is truth."
Joseph Fasano, author of *The Swallows of Lunetto*

"Gorgeous poems which seem to shimmer on that constantly shifting border between the body and the landscape."
Andrew McMillan, author of *pandemonium*

"From the beginning of the book to the end, the poet sets the reader's mind on fire with the luminous language, lyric intensity, and emotional heat of these poems. Patrick Errington's gorgeous, superbly crafted gems each shimmer under the poet's fierce gaze, and taken together achieve something grand and powerful."
Jennifer Franklin, author of *If Some God Shakes Your House*

THE HUGH MacLENNAN POETRY SERIES

Editors: Allan Hepburn and Carolyn Smart

Recent titles in the series

the swailing

PATRICK JAMES ERRINGTON

McGill-Queen's University Press
Montreal & Kingston • London • Chicago

ISBN 978-0-2280-1675-5 (paper)
ISBN 978-0-2280-1787-5 (ePDF)
ISBN 978-0-2280-1788-2 (ePUB)

Legal deposit second quarter 2023
Bibliothèque nationale du Québec

Printed in Canada on acid-free paper that is 100% ancient forest free
(100% post-consumer recycled), processed chlorine free

Funded by the Government of Canada · Financé par le gouvernement du Canada | Canadä | Conseil des arts du Canada · Canada Council for the Arts

We acknowledge the support of the Canada Council for the Arts.

Nous remercions le Conseil des arts du Canada de son soutien.

Library and Archives Canada Cataloguing in Publication

Title: The swailing / Patrick James Errington.

Names: Errington, Patrick James, author.

Series: Hugh MacLennan poetry series.

Description: Series statement: The Hugh MacLennan poetry
series | Poems.

Identifiers: Canadiana (print) 20220459312 | Canadiana (ebook)
20220459355 | ISBN 9780228016755 (softcover) | ISBN
9780228017882 (ePUB) | ISBN 9780228017875 (PDF)

Classification: LCC PS8609.R65 S93 2023 | DDC C811/.6—dc23

This book was typeset by Marquis Interscript in 9.5/13 Sabon.

For as long as anyone knows, people have had a ritual, every year, of setting fire to carefully controlled tracts of forest and field in an effort to limit the wildfires that otherwise sweep across the landscape. Fire to manage fire. This kind of controlled burn is sometimes called backburn, muirburn, or, in certain places, swailing.

CONTENTS

Contents

Contents

Here the long   edge
of town   Low
winter fog   my flesh
its gathering   A stand
of tamarack   or wind
-writhed   pine in the
distance   slow
ghosts   of a field
on fire   Silence
I want   so much
to say   My breath
my offering   We are
our bodies   burning

§

*Compare the phenomenon of thinking
with the phenomenon of burning ...*

You could come here and never arrive.
These towns like memories of towns,
all flecks of colour, barn-reds and brown
sinking into the haze of greys that no one

no matter how hard they try can quite draw
a word for (as if *any* word could draw this
like the bodies they drew from the almost-
iced-over river dripping up the bank

to be dried, identified, packed away).
You could leave, have left, and still wake
with water in your mouth, water instead
of a name. Each town's name peeling slowly

off sheet-metal siding or a rust-graffitied
bridge, as though picked at by the passing
vacant stares of commuters hurtling down
the 2A to the city. There can be no tense

imperfect enough for this. In every distance,
grain silos stand through the snow like steel
slivers of history that catch on the little light.
Like cracked teeth after a fight. Your tongue

will never rub them smooth. I'm not sure
you'd ever want to. But then again, I'm not
you (and you're welcome). Maybe though
you wouldn't mind – maybe just this once

you can let yourself off the hook, let some-
one else feel a way across your life, just once.
The girl behind the bar winces as she cuts
her palm on a nick in the old wood surface.

She smiles at you, briefly, from deep beneath
her face as she folds her bleeding hand
in a rag. Her blood is a dark hole in the ice
on a river we were all so sure we could skate on.

There's always one. Some slip
in the system, some grist folded in
with the flour, as your hands,
all sugar and slight, damasked
with bends, weave the requisite
meal from thin strings of pearl
millet, xanthan gum. Trust that
structure limits like, you think
sometimes, church windows limit
sunlight into colour. You know
it's not the same, though it accounts
for your never leaving, never
throwing down your life like
a bowl of fine wedding china.
Sequence perfects. Repeat it
to yourself. Sequence ... Until
it becomes a kind of quiet, silence
said but softly. Softly, you
wonder if all souls aren't bees
battering against the body's
windows. All bodies beating
against their breaths, their habits,
untouched glass. In the kitchen's
undivided sunlight, you measure
yourself against those little lies
you tell, whisked together,
molars of salt, distant spices,
almost perfect leavening. You stare

at your face in a countertop
that throws off all obligation
of light. Some night soon you'll slip
from here, from just beneath your life
to find you are precisely what you are.

SPOOKY ACTION AT A DISTANCE

In quantum physics, it has been theorised that entangled,
subatomic particles might somehow affect one another without
touching, regardless of the distance between them. Albert
Einstein, in disbelief, called it "spooky action at a distance."

Rain hushing the last of the light. The sort that seems
to touch everything – slate, lip, leaves – as if, by touching,

it might leave one last thing, this time, untold. In the last,
the word was *tender*. In the next, *spared*. In the last

lit flat across the street, I watch a couple wear their worn
orbits around each other: he dries, she puts each thing

away. Their hands never touch. Silence a tide between.
I think of my parents casting themselves like small coins
into what seas they wouldn't say. I wouldn't say

why I want to tell you this. Outside, a few drops drop in
the gutters. My neighbours I'll tell by lamplight and leavings,

binbags piling on the pavement, post that clots the door.
One word, one word, one word. One thing fitting always

precisely between, like birdsong fits what quiet may come
after this. Tell me there's just this world between us. That

you're there on the other side, hands pressed to the cold
of it. Can you feel that? Across the street & three floors

below, a man stoops as he steps out, as if by stooping
he might somehow make the drops stop head high.

Above all, he is careful. Unlacing the body,
a twine   white and patient as paper. His

is a process of exchange, a structure of one
for another, motion for motion, transaction.

In the cradle behind the ribs,   he plays
the horologist, unwinding the mechanisms,

the decay. He lines the vaulted organs, meticulous
as Murano glass, rasping out the rot. He has

always fancied himself a conservationist – But
he must work harder now, more quickly. The lung

next, the blood-sack economies depressed
beneath a haze of formalin. The heart-pocked

table is a scatter of excesses, indivisible
remainders. Wet boundaries of preservation

hardening. The glass begins to sweat, like – No,
there's no time left. The mouth, now – of course

the mouth, heaped beneath the face, shut
into an expression of averages. He sets the lips

for something, no,   not quite like speech.
Something harder, older. Feathers curl in the heat.

The eyes return each colour unused. Honey slips
between the sinews,   a reader returning one

last time. Loss finding what form it can keep.

SHRIFT

... and let there be laid on his body
iron and stone as much as he may bear,
or more ...

William Staunford, *Les Plees del Coron*, 1557

In dark and in secret,
they make love. Turning
wild as grain within

the windwork. There is
no wind. The room is

small. When he lowers
his mouth to her skin, it goes

smaller. Head bowed,
he admits her like a sentence
he has formed before,

many times, but only
now puts his voice to. As if
she were a confession.

His knees ache on the slate.
The house is a grey quiet
as a priest. No sound,

no shrift. If she breaks,
it is because she has
a body. If she breaks,

it's so there is nothing
to prove. There is nothing
but this for hours. Years

and a god ago, people
hauled the great sky
and slabs of stone up

from the river to a break
of aspen. Their bodies gleam

in the dark. They set a stone
on one man's chest, like
a hand, a comfort.

First one, then
another, then another.

Had I lain longer in the fire   break
between senses. Had colour   lingered,

patient, in the skin – already, the end
burns beneath the bed,   needles

out from the dark, veining the sheets
with a thin skein of fire. What animal

haunts the spelt, shivers
the broken stalks? Somewhere a lancet

of geese slits my chest like a skyline
bleeding winter.   Had I seared

my teeth apart, made a nest in the ash
of my mouth, would you have stayed?

HALF-LIFE

Babe, he calls me. Baby
Not long before. Even pet

Names decay. Well, they say
All leaves, once lit, fall, shed

For some barer season. I keep
My names like my baby teeth.

They rattle in the drawer next
To the bed. His tongue scours

My mouth. There are evenings
I watch the baring trees, frost,

Gather silence like a dark stone
In my mouth. Not absence but

Inverse of speaking. Colours
Recalled to cut glass. Late,

Later, I'll lay my love like
Leaves along the threshold.

When he calls, for half
The life of me, I will not turn.

Autumn, and everything is the last of its kind.
In this town, as in others, you grow up simply

because there is no other choice. Each morning is
an empty child's bedroom, the furniture dismantled
and set out in boxes on the lawn. I would tell myself

it's all for the best, if it were; better, maybe, better.
Evening comes hand-me-down, someone else's name

in felt-tip on the label. I find myself in this poem as
if sent to fetch something – I keep forgetting what.
It was important. I'm sure. My hands stammer

my pockets. Every finger is a thread worried free.
How long have I been standing here? Dishwater

gone cold up to the elbow. Through the window
the trees are raw as nerves and there are days I walk
in on myself as though caught naked. Days I feel

as if written, every movement measurable, every grief
just the name for grief. I remember reading, once,

that we take up a language and set the world to it.
All my old homes outgrow that word while winter
creaks in the stucco like a promise I broke to keep.

There could be worlds set, not to nouns, but to songs.
Love sounds, these days, so little like love, and some nights

I slip from beneath my vocabulary, move, barefoot,
between pools of unsung things spilled across the floor

like moonlight: The bedroom, kitchen (the blue
of the oven clock fingering the cutlery), the living
room, staircase, a long hall. If I could tell myself

I wouldn't. The quiet is a room without a purpose,
with nothing there to find, nothing to take back.

They told me as a child to be exact with pain.
Nurse it, they'd instruct, in the dark folds

of your brain, in the dirt and down. Let it seed, shiver
out, vein you, colour your skin like an empire

blushes a schoolroom map. I didn't listen. But I have
so much Alberta in me, my body, atlas

cedar at my core, bright as ribbon lightning, little
needled, now bare, now budding flame.
                              They've no words now,

but still a little breath, their mouths forgetting, sparks
for teeth. Listen. I'm setting down among my roots, ribs,

scarring for the scar I stem from. I can so nearly feel it,
like a last lost city, and a wild of fire gathered about my skin.

I'll make this a new mouth of me. Flames, like grackles
all ashiver along my lips. I have so much to tell you.

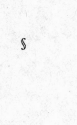

Watching, silent, another storm gather
along a far lip of hill, hesitate, then spill

over into the valley. Night somewhere,
coming swiftly. And something coming

little by little loose in me. A door left
unlatched. A word I can so nearly

recall ...   Windows stutter against
their frames. *You*. It must be. Or what I

still call *you*. That slight gap in the endless,
perfect elsewhere.
                    Rain beginning again, light

for now. Wind filling the chimney like a deep
breath. As though about to sigh, or speak out.

Say the silence grows around you, that the slip of light
is all that pins my hand to your chest when the senses quit
taking and start offering up the little blueabout, the little
stones they've culled from the riverbed. Say you're always

> *You, and a river's deepest turns promising your body*
> *a new shape, a way down. Orphan of water,*
> *step back onto the bent rocks, into*
> *the warming of me. There's too much sky,*
> *too much breathing to be done. You say I've never been*

small in the smallest room. Say sea. Say it backward
in my ear. Or instead say there's nothing left but
the nest of rust, that your body is emptied of you – how
wide your eyes say you can say everything, wildly, out,

> *wrong enough to be forgiven or forgive. Yet I bend,*
> *each night, to the sink as if to a nurse's hand,*
> *wait for the drought to wash me*
> *against the mirror. While you sleep, sometimes, I kneel*
> *on the cool tiles, hope they're white enough to take me in.*

like a chinook arch of thunderhead, hurling itself
against a field of bent gold, of canola flowers and tar,
until at night it admits stars. Or like a deer, god-split
on the snow, giving out a language of paling clouds.

Snow might come, but not without a break or a body
to collect against. If I could invent a word for a blank
square of my wall, would that make it real?
It can't exist, white, you told me. I've seen snow only
from the shadows, said you by saying everything you are not.

Its marrow sucked from the open ulna until it draws
crystals of cold to the muzzle. Say you said
it all, your colours to the coils of your fingerpads,
what would you let light? Finches. Copper wire. Rome.
Caraway. You. Say none of this never happens.

All day in the heat they would talk. Some even
sang, though no one could hear the others'
words through the grit and noise, the blackened
grind of machinery. But still they'd drive their
voices like fenceposts into the hard din of it,
not a fence for keeping in some untamed
thing, but rather just the plain act of keeping.
As a boy, I used to cross the fields to watch
them at it, the sweat, their mouths moving as
practiced as their hands, shaping the steel dust,
the air – into what, I could never quite say.
A craft of some sort, of sound, of stale light.
Whenever my father came home he'd leave
the keys dangling in the pickup, a scum of grey
around the bath and, every now and then, her
(my mother, I mean), driving with me away
for days, weeks even, but we always came and
were taken back. I guess he liked the act of it,
leaving. I still remember him mumbling along
to the radio, but at home he never sang, not
to anyone, barely spoke in more than those
sentences he set out on the table, cruel little
heirlooms. My mother who spoke enough
for all of us told me how she eventually had
to ask him to stop saying he loved her, and so
he did, though as he neared the end she'd hear
him at night muttering the words and her name
over and over as though they were a kind of
work he'd done all his life and now his breath,

like his hands, was set to it. I could always tell
as he and I drove back that we were almost home
when, though we kept no cattle, no horses,
the untended fields were scored with fences.

So you find yourself in another night without winter,
slipping inside the fabric of some hand-me-down

life. Beside you, you can sense the mass of it, living,
all haunches bulked against you, all coarse hide

in your mouth. There's nothing to say. As you lead
it down the hall by a horn, feet sticking to hardwood,

little light scattered like broke china across the moteless,
motionless space, you scrawl your senses over the picture

frames, the measureless dark of small bedrooms, stuccoed
skies. Listen to a round snap of hooves that trails you,

until you step free onto the outgrown lawn, relishing
the gasp of frost in the webbing of your toes. But still

the moon comes muffled by the streetlamps that buzz

in their glass hives, drooling honey. Your breath scrapes,
fogging the cold like starlings, you imagine, school

up from the pitch of a hawk. You consider how years of
quiet hold you together like a mould you never fill, still

wondering at the depths beneath the crests of houses
around you. Seas, you decide, as you turn back to yours,

follow the two sets of prints, sense the door closing
fast above you, fitting its frame, flawed, not like water.

I might have been beautiful. Let me be
a while yet. Stay. Tell it again. Please,
so close your skin frays the cotton slip
of morning over us. All night we wished

each other into being, budded out like
furred new antler, like fingers trawling
the air. Winter, then. But still I flowered
first teeth along the jawbone. We spoke

each other almost solid, word replacing
world, bit by bit: hand, hoof, human, hart.
A story said to still another story. A life
dreamt in the glass city of a dictionary,

each reflection needing another, every
mechanism needing measure, each grief
a god, until at last we find it: some first
light shaken loose from the mirror, heart

folded free from pages, eyes filling like
sails: a great, fenceless wild taking hold
our hands in its hands, plunging them deep
in earth, as if to tell us, *Not here, not here – here.*

MOTEL

Thin sheets, thin walls, thin
skin. Feint of the Victorian

in the lampshade, the last
occupant's hair in the sink.

The single room holds you
like a child

might hold up one small
smooth stone. You don't mean

to think that, but you do.
Each thing can be thought

as something else. Remember
that. The radiator, a comfort. Guilt –

Would there weren't this river
beneath the bed. Maybe then,

maybe then. An ambulance
sobs. The sound smears the walls, the

carpet. It's okay. There's
a mirror for you to wash upon

as though it were a riverbank.
Your body, its confession.

Not all things
can be forgiven. On the bed,

the sheets a catastrophe of white.
You slip under them, under

your breath, the current,
unnoticed, and unlooked for.

THE CALL

Every morning through the clay dawn
we'd watch them drawn down the hill
to the city. Not seeking anything, not at least
as far as either of us could ever tell (a bell
sounding somewhere in the distance),
bringing nothing back, their hands like
rainwater at their sides. As if their own
absence drew them, the way even quiet
seems to draw a sound to still it. I still don't
know what draws me back to this. My hands
a whisper along on the walls as if feeling
for a door. A mumble of rain constant
in the eaves, filling in the silence, spilling
over. Does the Tao say a bell's emptiness
is its use? When she left, what came wasn't
emptiness but a species of excess, as though
somehow I'd filled into and then one day
over the loss of her, moving constantly, foot
to foot, room to room like water running over
eaves and thinking of those nights emptying
ourselves into each other, and later watching
as outside they'd climb the hill, step
by step again each into their own shadow,
and a bell, maybe? And all at once I'm glad
I can't say for sure. As if there's some
small space left, a silence that might still
call for sound, for prayer, for poems, for

LONG LAST

Maybe it is the very last of days. Last summer light
longing the telephone lines. And here you are

a kid, just shy maybe of seven, allowed at long
last to join in the game, hidden, all giddy and grin, breathless

in the uncut grass well beyond the last vacant row of houses,
lying on your back, fists full of turf and the darkening

sky pressed tight against your face. You shouldn't be
out this late – your body athrill, undiscovered, others long

since gone in. Someone should be calling you home. Hold
your breath. Any second now. But not yet. Not just yet.

§

The tongue also is a fire ...

KWASHIORKOR

Had I eaten my fill of you I might have lived.
The creatures that take inheritance of me
would have gone hungry without any help,
bellies bloated for the lack. Might now
be baring too-bent bodies to the heaving sky
as it grinds through the pelts for the meat –
even the sun is starved round. Eating was a poor
relief, it seems. Because I did eat. Ate
everything: the whitewash off the walls down
to the baseboards. Chewed my elbows
to the gristle, joists, stripped the world to
clear colour, deserts sluicing out until all
to see was veined red. Then ate root into
the dirt and lay there in the furrow looking up.
Had I sacrificed to each other my little mammal
hands, would that have sated? Had I grown
greater on what you hollowed out would you
have stopped offering? Had I slit myself
down the middle, let in the famished air, is there
some thing left in me that might fly out?

THEY DON'T MAKE GODS
FOR NON-BELIEVERS

When I tell him I'm dying, my doctor says I'll die
years and years from now if I'm careful, so I will

die, then, I say, but carefully. After all, if it's worth
doing then it's got to be worth doing carefully

and my doctor agrees (he should). All the same
you *can* be too careful, which is why I see him far less

than is, quote-unquote, prudent. My doctor, I mean, not
God. Him, I see so much more than should a devout

non-believer. But never where I expect to – great
storms, great losses, and the like. Rather in the pale

residues left by latex gloves, or the soft patience
of a painkiller. Maybe that's a sign I'm approaching

the end. Or it may just be the perfunctory depression
of my tongue again, the requisite ah. Ah, as though

comprehending. But let's face it, comprehension's
not the issue. I mean, I can comprehend, like glass,

that light with all its grit and sine comes apart
into colour but that hardly warms this halogen, hardly

amounts to *understanding*. My doctor thinks his is
a look of understanding, with all that plastic wisdom

of sign and symptom, but understanding nothing
of mine. Between you, me, and my god, my God

I've got a lot to cower from. Which, I guess, means
I should put faith in one of us. But Him I don't trust

any more than my doctor, or me, or any more
than anyone else so reliant on terror in their acolytes,

shivering and braille-skinned, deaths confessed to
and calendared. He laughs at my swithering, hands

swaddled in the too-white light, reading my body,
asking who I'll speak to when I write this, kneeling,

pages closing more careful than hands on the bed.

What the fuck do you know
About dying? she's asking, taking
My hand and placing it inside
Her wrist. What does *anyone*?

(I'm drunk, and it's hard not to be
Sarcastic in such situations.) But
Then I feel the scars, trace one
With my finger, pale and raised

Like her voice. For one reason
Or another, I like that she calls it
Dying, as if death were an act,
A skill you could practice, learn

By heart, perfect. I have, I should
Tell you right now, never tried
Dying (won't go giving my parents
More excuses to call me a failure,

To chalk up my whole life as dying
Unsuccessfully). I do though collect
Deaths in the drawer with the dead
Batteries, twist-ties I swear I'll use

Someday, with the dark pebbles
I still keep in my pockets, turning
Over and over until I've worried
Away all the rough edges, all

The scars. Her wrist won't stay
Smooth beneath my hand, her life
Snagging in her skin. Later and
Alone, the bars closed and even

The streetlights all slicked
Black, I catch my toe in the
Cracked pavement and nearly
Fall. The pain cuts a small
White smile across my face.

I prithee, be my god.

The Tempest II.ii

Despite all my efforts, no god will stay
still for me for long. Like a child, comfortless
in the backseat as we drive home, maybe after

seeing her first movie, the trip immeasurable, what
with her wild imagining. I'll never have
that child, but I can imagine her and like to

think that's why I still catch myself praying
to some great, invented imaginer, though I don't
technically believe in one. Imagine

how utterly alone that first creature
(I picture, for some reason, a whitetail deer
standing, sudden, in the morning light)

must have felt in a forest of only thought-of
things. Like reading a book that, without
warning, mentions you by name. I think of one

god sat alone in a bedroom, scattered around
with toys, a whole heaven of posable, actionless
Action Men (no batteries, of course, included).

Just imagine the surprise at finding yourself
invented, called on – first by one, then another,
then endlessly, and for some

reason, I think of that child again, asleep now,
as the grey miles slide into the wild beyond
the headlights. She's fidgeting a little, like coffee

in a to-go cup, a dream somehow restless
within the reality of things, the seat, the snow-
flickered woods, the plain life, the dark.

I can hear them but only just
make them out, the kids

slouching there at the far end
of the one long road, the long

end of the light. Sunlight,
dust, more than enough

to wear away whatever
pull this town might've had

once, signs of – call it *life, colours,
clues*. I have no fucking clue

why I keep coming back, year
after year – not drawn here, not

driven, but each night I dream
of rivers, water taking

whatever will give
of the ground. This ground,

this town, hell, it'll give –
has given. Given

everything. & those kids,
there, shoulders set

against another for-sale
shopfront – I can't even

tell which is holding up
which. But something must,

this place, my place, & the wind
off the mountains giving

way the wideness of the world.
That's being generous,

I know. But I'll give it
that. I'll give.

HALF MEASURES

It's been years, now, since she left and even
still he sleeps on just half the bed. After all,

it really is easier to make that way, quicker
to hide all evidence of dreaming, like photographs

hastily put back up on the shelf. He's become
a tenant of fractioned closets, of half-portioned

recipes, of refracted light. He sometimes tells
himself, like time, there is managing in measure,

absence held in the hand-span, the half-heart,
the hair's breadth. For comfort, he remembers

seeing the great Dutch paintings – Dou, sometimes
Vermeer – the immeasurable lives made so nearly

bearable in the frame, slightness like a bird's
body in a plastic bag. As a child, he used to

count miles on telephone poles while, in front,
his parents spoke in weather-levelled voices.

When he'd told her this she pitied him. When
he would add up all the countries he wanted to

show her, she'd tell him that numbers are such
a man's way of holding the world, but, when

women love, they love innumerably. Softly,
he'd said he only wanted to hold her. He'd never

admit how, against her body, he felt so desperately
proportionate, how sometimes he would lie

along the bathroom tiles as though the seams
and scale would make him somehow bearable

as a painting, would hold him. Not because
he needed holding, but maybe just to know loss

could be travelled, as he watched planes scrawl
across the unbound blue through the window.

So often, these days, he thinks of grief in terms
of distance. Carefully plotting out the lengths

involved in the longing, he imagines himself some
ancient philosopher slowly dividing the distance

toward home, thinking of a child's hands, still
sticky with the juice of a poorly-divvied fruit.

How impossibly small it all can seem, small
like distance, halved, and halved, and halved again.

Don't worry. This isn't the beginning. I know
you, I know how you worry about all that is
to come and so do I, and that's fine. This has,

at least, been written now, the page turned to
maybe once or twice before, these little letters all
shaped on someone's tongue. Aren't colours

really light revised in the eye? All these years
you've been buried in your life, whittled roots
into woodwork, set windows in walls, and all

the while thoughts scuffle in the skirting board.
Yours is a familial place, though no one else
has dug into this moment before. But familiar

to you as your mother's elbows, grandfather
clock, heirloom tomatoes. All these blue hours
spent pacing the hall as if it were a throat,

scrubbing the old floorboards down to dirt,
scouring your hands thin just for some sound,
vowelless, fricative – *Shh*. Don't be afraid.

You've known far too long what it is to love
a closed door. And how to knock. It's time
you did some speaking. There's a sea out there

calling for its name. Don't worry about me.
What's left is just revision, just working out
the pitch, like a gull hones sharp the angle

of the plunge beneath the wing. Shorelines amending
themselves to the tide. Or, the way each line lies
flat upon the last (this is not the last), each life

accounts for its loss, each word cradles its
extinct species. Or, more like how the last
time you left, I knew where to meet you.

COLD: EXCHANGE

If there's anything to get from what's lightless
it's less space, the world crowding in to touch
and breath. Right now in a plot of north

Canada, exposure alone is sufficient
to strip a drunk down to the body, but here
I'm frayed far from mine by the scrabble

of sheets on sleeplessness. Not much
as problems go, when people are dying
just outside my language, and try

as I might there are so many that elude
still the word for comfort as I stretch it
over the page like a hand, feel into the gut

beyond the human, groping down to dumb
mammal warmth. The distant country across
the mattress answers me in absence like

the quiet behind the door yawns
for you: cold, it tells me, and I shiver out
from under snow and sleep and no matter

how I churn, blink the frost from my eyes,
press my heart beyond me into things,
still this word, still this small word.

§

Pray, lord.
We are near.

1. Vignette Study, January

Cold wasting a way through your open coat.
Drunk, stumbling against a fence, against a word.
Shiver. Hoarfrost. Trying to recall the way back
as if it were some half-forgotten language, trying
to remember if its speakers spoke of the past
as behind them or ahead. Or above. Above,
heaven is an unspeakable history of snow. Roads
and windrows gathering in great tomes of it. Birds
in the distance, rising, like a cloud of breath, or maybe
myth. You wonder where they could be going
at this hour. Home. You can almost picture it.
Copse of poplar and a clearing sky and something
else just beyond. You could see it if you'd only
try. If you just close your eyes. Just for a minute.

2. Field with Missing Figure

Not a field so much as an accident of foxtail
between two roads, a mutter of trees and snow
like a scab itched to scar, as if the sky too can't
quite leave it be. I'm trying now almost daily
to leave that place in the hope of coming back
to find it beautiful. Without your body, without
having to wonder how anyone could've let you walk
home drunk, the wrong way into January, how
someone must have seen you there and slowed maybe
briefly before telling themselves, He'll be fine, some-
one will take care of him, and driving on. My mother
mentions you every time we drive past and I'm sure
she sees my body there as much as yours. In the bare
trees, a sudden static of birdwings like an ill-tuned TV.

3. *Sunset, Sylvan Lake, Alberta*

It's almost too warm for once. Heat pleading
me from me, whining sweat out of the skin,
another breath from the body, and you back
out of that winter. I hate that it has become
somehow strange to remember you alive. Even
in poems, I can't seem to see past your death,
as though inside at night with the lights on trying
to tell what's moving on the lawn. But it's summer
now and the lake allows heaven a bit closer to home.
I can imagine you here, so fiercely alive it must be
a memory. And you're speaking, telling me how
if you just unfocus your eyes a little, look past
the water, you can sometimes catch the faintest
flicker of fish as they rise to ripple heaven like rain.

4. *Self-portrait as Possibility*

I'm not really surprised your parents moved away.
The past gets caught up in things, like twigs
or bits of rubbish trapped in a sewer grate
when the snow starts to melt. Parks filling up
with runoff and children splashing about, birds
in rubber boots, trying to find flowers. Little chance
of rain these days, little need. I never learnt who
found your body, who plucked you up out of winter –
I wonder if they tried to warm you against their body,
how long did they hold you? I've replayed that scene
so long it should've melted away. But things catch in me.
One day I'll end up dreaming I was the one to find you,
but still alive this time, still in a thicket of life, bird-smile
lit on your lips. I hold you the way the sky holds rain.

5. Landscape Without

It's raining, the sky and all its apologies collapsing in
around me and, on days like today, I can't see the point
in blaming anything. I was hoping to call you back without
abstraction, without making you something you are
not. But you're dead and the dead are just symbols
that have taken the place of the living, the way
the word for loss might in time take the place
of loss. Some small noun of me believes that. Some
thing in me thinks if I, whatever today's rain, just
say snow again, say shiver, say wind-stripped tree and
twitch of birds again, of birds, of birds, again of birds –
well, no one dies in a poem, right? No one freezes to death
in the word *field*, no matter how cold. I will tear apart
every dictionary for whatever name called you from you.

6. Untitled Sketch, Afterward

Snow now, getting thick. Light, milk light, the house
sopping with it. No post again today and none likely
the next. I don't mind. I can get by on this: cold
coffee, cable news, a cup of stale water for the pills
beside the bed. Losing by list and leftover, less
and lessening. Missing, each morning, a little more
appropriately. No birds. Not this time. Days pass like
(why do I keep thinking this?) a pickup truck down
a lampless dirt road. I can't sleep for dreaming it. And
something (someone?) out there in the dark, the dry
grass gone still with snow and a last truck flickering
by (why isn't it slowing?), its sound thinning smoke
(why won't it stop?) and its taillights embers (stop –
please) going grey, going out, going, going –

7. *Preparatory Study for Whatever Is to Come*

Snow again, and after. The water left out last night un-
touched in its bowl as I step outside, the cheap tin door
scraping its small soul shut behind me. I know, I know.
I don't believe in ghosts. The world's far too full
for that. Especially on days like this, the field bird-
less, brimming. For a long time, what I feared was a kind
of emptiness, writing you somehow out. I thought of your
mother some day, month, year finally bringing herself
to pour out the water she'd set that night by your bed.
I can still see her moving about the house, every shelf,
every room unbearably ordered, untouched, exactly
as she left it. It's getting cold again; I should go in.
For a second, above, I feel some feathered thing stir, not
quite written. I stop. Then I fill the bowl again. Set it out.

§

All things are an exchange for fire ...

They set out again before dawn, in the quarter light, eighth
light, so early I can't be sure they had ever really stopped.

No candles, torches – what they must tell they tell by touch.
Wince of rime, disused machinery. Wheatgrass wished along

a wrist. That's as much as they'll tell me, at least – I have
no reason not to take them at their word: Rust. Shiver. Bone.

I can tell they're out there, darker upon the dark. But I can't
say why it is tonight, of all nights, that I find myself falling

into step, half-step, behind, hoarfrost folding in each
footfall, in each eyelash as I blink. Loon-call of a freight

train fathoming the valley behind. Ahead, they've stopped.
Don't ask me how I know. How many of them are there.

Of us. The quiet quickening, the darkness like a hand
to hold me back. No telling what from. In the barn some-

where to my left, I can hear what must be a horse pawing
the dust for nothing. There – the heft of it, ache of sweat

in its coat, each hair twisting between my fingers. I can't say
for sure it is there but something must be, something –

And then the first match is lit. The night ripped open white.
This life later, I still can't say why it is we did it, every year,

burn the fields bare, to ash, to bedrock. I asked only once, as
a boy, my father's hands still thick with work. He didn't turn

from the sink but told me, as if (I think now) only telling
will keep some thing untold: *It was always going to burn.*

Come on, out with it, my father calls over his shoulder, over
his breath, barks it, breaking off the words like dead

twigs – *Spit it out* – like the action figure I'm holding broken.
Tell it like it is. Like it is? Me, shaking there, six and sparrow

in the hawk of him, in the shadow of the garage he's always
fixing. Silence a hand over my mouth. I want nothing

like it is. I want the blood that will, later, billow blue
beneath my left eye like stormclouds. I want his hands,

even now, want wind-bent wheat, body antlered light.
Want that morning, not any of the others, some kind of

kindness, air swollen with it, snow that won't
come, that never comes. *Come on, boy*, he calls me

like a dog. But something else steps from the storm.

NOT AN ELEGY

You are dead and the dead are very patient.

Jack Spicer, After Lorca

Thank fuck there's still a little weather left. Snow,
Which means you don't have to talk about it, means
Despite itself, no poems needed. That said, outside

The beech trees are making metaphors for you, and
In the hallway the light seems to feel some need to fill
All the corners like water, as if some losses wouldn't be

Happy left lost. But they'll be fine, right? I mean, sure,
You still have to wear a language, like a Walmart uniform
All creases and unwashed rigid, but it doesn't mean you

Have to say anything. The words can serve themselves
For a change, wandering in the aisles, all want without
What. Of course they can't help but mean no matter

The mechanism but what's to say they have to mean
Him? Nothing, that's what; he's for the line you meant
This to be. For today, screw it, it's snowing, stay in. Eat

Your Wheaties dry. In this sentence no one has to die.
And there's weather enough for a few more. With luck
It'll keep a while, keep up. Even if you can't help wondering

When you'll actually dig a real poem out of this. Yes, you
Know that will mean him, mean leaving the weather hollow
Like a bell. And hey, some say it's the empty part that rings.

But it's best left later. Save all that for the next draft, with
Your better metaphors, standing, half-lit in the hallway,
For everything they're not, the snow meaning wildly beyond.

That one will mean admitting him, what he is. But it is
So late now and this poem's ending, settling into nouns like
Nothing. Someday, you'll admit *you* almost always
    means *me*.

WHEN THE DOCTOR TELLS HIM HER CANCER IS BACK, *I SEE*, MY FATHER SAYS, AND HANGS UP

> ... *seeing ye shall see,*
> *and shall not perceive.*
>
> Matthew 13:14

Barely beyond the last of the houses when we stop.
The Dodge pulled in tight to the fence, letting
passing cars shudder past.   I follow
my father's finger
                    first to his lips, then across
to the side window, to the sky, the all too wide
world pressed white against the glass. I didn't see them,
not at first. The day so thin a breath might break it.
                                        Then
one,
        another. Rising from the frozen field like waves
of it. Eyes black loam, antler
                            bared clay. Breath
foaming in air.   I recall them so clearly now, so
exactly, but I must've seen dozens by that age, dozens
certainly since.
                The quiet gathering.

                                When I turned back
to him, he was staring straight ahead, down the now vacant
highway, gathering nothing. His hands white to the wheel.

I meant to say something and maybe meaning drew him to himself. *Right*, he said, or I think he said, voice folding into the silence. *Let's go*.

 And we did. The deer folding into distance behind, and we into whatever it was we were to be.

INHERITANCE

You've had that dream again. You know the one
        that wakes you. You rise to rough wood floors, doors

that only ever open in, whining away as if they could
    blame you
        for wanting to leave. But you're alive
          and can't help feeling

forgotten, somewhere in your body like a wreck in deep
        water. When you walk out to your car, the grey
          light is shot

with green and salt, your senses pressing so heavily
        around you it gets hard to breathe. And even the
          sky weighs

enough these days to crush the best of 'em. You sometimes
        hear what sounds
          like small bones splinter. Come on,

be reasonable, think it through. It hurts every time
    you think of it
        and of this unhorsed town no one really grows up
          in, the greys

and the one bar that every evening seems to lead to
    like the numbers
        on a clock that's always a little behind the time.
        Isn't this the life

you asked for? The hand-me-down that had looked so good on
      your big brother worn thin
         on you now, your shoulderblades,

ribs like the substation your brother's friends haunted
      as kids, consecrating it with pilfered beer and piss.
         But you made it

your temple, imagining what gods once hummed in the wiring,
      the rituals, the sacrifice. But even then you'd begun
         to find yourself

beneath your senses, your body just some house you
   inherited, never
      really yours. The taste of iron rusting
        in the synapse, the touch come apart

at the seam. You know there are people in foreign countries,
      their language reaching, right now, like a hand for
        your life,

their voices like rain along a windowpane, pooling on the sun-
       sealed dirt, the husks of wheat, the wind piled against

the baseboards. When the TV goes out, when the lights let slip
      their shadows, for a moment you can nearly
        feel someone. You wonder what,

if not you, will reach back when you wake in the dark.
      Just who do you think you are?

There's nothing to distinguish
this from the last three-or-so
hundred fields they pass, but
for whatever reason they call it
far enough. The engine shaking
free its sound, voices streaming
from their mouths to the ground.
When they say *let's go* they won't
mean everyone, this time. Beyond,
a field frozen solid, expression-
less, stubbled with broken grain.
They'll leave him loose as teeth
in his life, lashed to a fencepost.
Blood gently unlacing the features
from his face and every wound
unwinding from its pain like wire.
It'll be days before anyone can tie
the term *missing* to what it has
to mean. The field and his flesh
grow significant against their will.

There's a sense that what is left
is somehow *more* than what is left
off. That whatever remains must be
the point, like the point he carves
of each fencepost before driving them
into the frost-hardened dirt. Steam
streaming from his hands into the long
dawn light as he pulls off his gloves,
wipes the dust from his lips. That night,
face smeared across the bathroom
mirror, he'll slowly undress, peeling
away the sweat-stiff shirt and jeans,
and with them the day, all its
gathered pain, each wince and hiss.
He'll touch his body then, softly
testing it with the tips of his fingers,
pressing into the skin, the scars, as
though he were some not-yet-named
world. He'll take off his wedding ring,
set it beside the sink. And then
the rest. All of it. Everything he can
be without – hair, tooth, hand, limb by
limb, scraping, scouring away, cutting
down, knowing he will find it, has
to find it, that pure thing that is left,
the sharp point of him, what he
is, just a little farther now, he thinks,
a little beneath, the water running
dark down the drain. In the morning

he'll head back out before dawn,
a stack of new posts shuddering in
the truck. It's just ahead, he can tell
and he stops, steps from the cab, here
where he left off. But there's nothing.
No fence. No post. Nothing. Or not
quite nothing. A line of deep holes,
stretching off into the half-light, each
one perfectly round and full of water.

FIRE, CATCHING

The way the damasked wings
around an elm seed seem, for just
a moment, to catch on a little ledge
of air, turning up and over, hanging
there. The way this late summer
light might snag, tangling itself
in knots of nettle, switch grass, wild
raspberry, or how that first flame splits
itself open along a sharp, curled edge of
birchbark. The way it gathers, as elm
keys gather against the porch, the lip
of the cheap screen door, the hall already
dark beyond, as someone near leans back
into the moment and the evening lies
flat across the lawn saying *Isn't this
the fucking life?* And it is the life, this life,
this, here, this thing catching on the air.

MEASURES OF CONTAINMENT

I'm flickering through
yet another dozen-
odd pictures posts
re-posts boasting *all*
the things that can be
done while staying
home – virtually
anything apparently diy
sourdough *stay home*
save lives –
each life displayed
in its little box each
loss in its careful
counted characters &
sometimes I worry
that so much can
be contained like
this in a screen
a home a poem maybe
the way a body can
be said to contain
its pain everything
you are in a life
-time meaning in
a word & for what
-ever reason I wish
& wildly to let it
out just once let
life exceed the body

that   lives   it   let
wild   let   the   line   *this*
line   maybe   reach   just
a   bit   too   far   to   the   ...
but   what   if   I   have
the   word   wrong   what
if   it's   not   so   much   *in*
but   maybe   *through*   &
by   *through*   I   mean   less
in-one-side-out-the-other
less   *beyond*   than   *by*
way   *of*   or   maybe
even   *with*   &   for   what
-ever   reason   I   wish
&   wildly   for   a   way   of
reaching   out   to   you
a   hand   with   which
to   tell   you   that
whatever   it   is   what
-ever   you   are   going
through   right   now
you   can   you   will
live   through   this

What more
to say? What

of this snow
-rankled sky?

This low lie
of comfort some

pale lip on these
car-furrowed streets

these towns strewn
with what should be

called living but
isn't. Even wolves

curl around their
rocking hearts

to sleep.
Eventually even

I will leave you
be as you ask.

$\int$

If you look close, everything moves. But it's not enough.
The party winding down around you – your ears humming

to fill in where the voices have turned back, atoms of air
taking their cues from the cars on a wet street three stories

below. Tell yourself there's sometimes quiet. You are still
in the wild of your life, senses bringing news of winter

and departing. There's a glass of water in front of
    you, ringing
the table, gathering up the warmth from your palm.

Each particle furiously staunching another. Consider
that waxwings wake in the cold. It is not enough to take

place. An event of viridian in the grass. There's no keeping
anything together. Your body packs the wound it makes

in the grey field as you walk toward home. As the
    door closes
behind you, another day bleeds itself dry across the snow.

The same long dirt strip of road holds me
like a breath as the evening gathers, folds
over, pulls me in and down. Darkness
in fathoms against my ears, my chest. I can taste
the silt in it, glacier. *It'll be* – what I wouldn't
give for someone to say – *okay*. I know these
back roads like a mother tongue – the rhythm,
the roll of them, the feel. I can't help thinking
of someone coming home in the dark, alone, one
hand closing the door as the other feels along
the bare wall for the light. No light tonight,
nothing past the pickup's one good beam, the
whispers of snow that slither through the gravel
to gather in windrows just there out of sight.
The scenic route. That's what you used to call
this. The sky empty, the fields somehow emptier.
On clear days, you would swear you could see
the mountains along the horizon. I could swear
I can feel them now, hunched there, that bulk
holding this whole place together, dark against
dark. I have been trying so fucking hard to hold
this together, not the image but the feel of you
here, beside me in the back seat, our faces
pressed against opposite windows, the same
huge dark just beyond. I can't help thinking
of the river that must by now be somewhere
just to my left, how we used to play that game,

taking turns to feel our way as far as we could out
onto the ice. How we loved the thrum of water
just under us. How some things, for a long time,
for such a long time, hold. And then they don't.

They've been telling her over and again to speak
about it. If not to them well then to someone, no
one, even. Get it into words. That old saying

about how a mountain can only be moved one
little stone at a time. After all, we say *flower*
to hold this writhing into colour. I say nothing

as she invites me into a room strewn with them.
As she shuts the door quick against the wind, moves
off to make tea. Nothing as a minute later I hear

a cup shatter across the kitchen floor, as I hear
then a door open, close. Hear what sounds like
someone scream once, wildly into the storm. And still

nothing, as storm becomes stillness, as she comes in
again, takes the dustpan from me. As she wraps each
piece by piece in tissue, places them in the bin. Still

a cup, despite everything. We sit for a long while, her
and me, not moving, each word rolled smoother
than any stone in my mouth. Her grief like no

flower in this world. *Don't worry,* she says when I,
later, pick up my coat to leave. *I'll manage.* For every
word, there is, I know, another. For every sentence,

at least one reads only *no no no no no no no.*

Enough first bread and forgetting. Enough tearing
    back wisteria
from the window frame. Enough letting go (enough
    going). It's alright

to keep a place on the shelf, the set-aside silverware,
    the light lit,
all night, on the porch. But enough putting things off,
    sweeping

crumbs beneath the skirting board, the heirloom rug,
    whatever
living it is you do these days. Enough watching the news
    three days

late, letting the past just be the past, leaving things
    well enough
alone. Enough envy for birds, for impossible blues,
    for leaving

everything behind. You can't keep ignoring the deer prints
    in the yard.
Enough answered prayers, enough bequeathing: time
    should be kept

wild and untold and untelling. Like the field behind
    your childhood
home, gathering the sky off the windows as you grew.
    Leave a door

unlocked, just in case. Leave all the beds unmade, enough
bric-a-brac
to come back for. Stop trimming your longest longings
back. Enough

enough, altogether. And no mirrors, no touch rinsed off
your hands,
no more hands described as bare, unfeathered wings
(there are things

worth holding). Enough putting back what you find.
I cannot manage alone.

GLEANING

On hands and knees, we take what we call
the middle ground. If a god can be found
here, it's because he couldn't commit either,

combing, like waves, the shingle, wanting
just some scrap worth settling on. Life,
at least, has settled on your body like silt

on that wreck no one survived. When
you, daily, wake, it's as if washed ashore.
When you wish, it's a hundred life-rafts'

beacons swimming in the dark. Imagine
a language where these are no different.
You pray and it's enough. Instead you lie

awake, knotting sheets, small hours heaped
up like driftwood. You could manage, make
do, get by, and you can. But there's a loss

for every light, for every sense's salvage.
Just to be alive to this world is an act of war.
You know to take a hand, some small thing

will go unheld. Only hands keep their losses
from reclamation. Only in this language
is the sky something less than heaven.

THIS WAS SOMETHING MORE

Was ours. Was the thing found spelt on the back
    of our mother's knees. Was what called you

    a bird. Was what took my mouth for home. Was
rain and rain then until rain became

quiet brought close. Was a kind of speaking,
    you said, was means of giving up. Breath keeping

    time between the teeth. Was managed now,
was loss was dirt. Was not dirt. Was the darker thing. Was

home built on home, was notion set
    on bone. Was wind come to plead

    at our window, asking, asking. Why I planted
wilderness around us and called it flesh. Was

roots taking dirt as my branches took you. Was
    night too not falling, growing from our feet. Was

    this last lie to a brother. Was the wind everywhere,
a whine in the wattle-work. Was the burl box

you recall, or was my body you carved
    into your palms. Was the wind leaving

    just this stand of sycamore for shelter. Was
whispered, now, was you. I assume you.

Was this tremor in the dark, this managing
        of air. Was getting by. Was the tithe or

        leave-taking. Was spoken around you still
as wind. Was have and haven't. Was what I

promised you. What I couldn't keep. Was
        winnowing. What the wind cannot ask, but was

        answered. Was birds. Was threat set loose
this shriek of starlings from the gloom. Was

wonder. Wondered then. Was now. Was never. Was
        this wind, this wind working you. Was not

        weathered, but worn. Was wear. Was you told
me once, not grief. Not grief, safekeeping.

AUGURY

That is to say: language is not predicated on the existence
of meaning, but is an unpredictable outcome of a world that
produced first fire, then birds.

Andrew Joron, *The Cry at Zero*

It doesn't mean that I miss you somehow
less these days, these days growing
numbers like new leaves – there won't,
I know, be leaves, not for months yet.
The creek bed I cross to class tenders
stones to sky. Shop windows tender frost.
Means today will be short, tomorrow
shorter. Means just a little more
of heaven for whatever birds are left
between the branches. I don't know
anymore, who I mean this for. *Mean*, as
in *intend*. In some vast distance a man watches
fire tend his field. In class, my students tend
to elsewhere, eyes flocking up and away.
I can read the signs, dot to dot, trace
paths of flight, patterns of migration.
I should call them back, but I won't.
Every hour, on the hour, they rise,
a rush of feathers, *thank yous*, *see yous*,
sorrys. I know. I know. Every minute to
measure, longing to line. *It's okay*,
I want to say, as bags swing, jackets flap,

doors stammer. *It's all okay.* I want
so much to mean it. More the gesture
than the words. A small species of tenderness,
a reaching out that might be letting go.

For days it seemed like it would rain, though it never did.
Fraying October sky all agrasp as if in a foreign language,

as if soil & slate & skin were terms it had learnt once in
grade-school maybe &, unpractised, forgot. I'm forgetting

who it was I'd meant to tell this to. The words coming bit
by bit apart against the air. I can feel whole vocabularies
of you, just there, past this language, this line. I've heard it

said that one particle can feel another turning, turning
even on opposite ends of the universe, & I hold to that

as something like hope. As if somehow just wondering
might be enough. Days like these, I can't help but wonder

about my mother, about the wince that flickered across
her face when I raised my hand, leaving, to wave goodbye.

She used to tell me how much I had come to look like him,
my father, & I do, though we left him our whole lives

ago. As if I had grown like sharp wood into the wound
of him. Bare elms fit each flaw in the sky. The sky

tonight is clear & irrevocable, each & every thing laid out
beneath like heirloom silverware. Tell me, whoever you are,
whoever you are. Tell me you've saved one small thou

of you. In a window across the street, a woman I'll never
meet lights a single, naked lamp, & all the stars go out.

LOW TIDE AT THE END
OF THE PEFFER BURN

I

Even ending was animal. A tide pulled back
over mudflat. Softening interstices. Little definitions

lighting upon the scene from the easy tongues
of air, image teased here

                              and there apart.

This early light wholes things. Wet bursts
of presence: ghost shrimp
in their consistent burrows, goby, eelgrass.

The insistence of a dragonfly's compound eye.
No shapes but signs

                              of life.

                                        A worm avoids

a plover's stab. Pools wash themselves
in wind.   Instance assured

by a recurrence of waves. Lineations
of salt mark what has drawn back into itself;
a paper-white that permits all colour.

Leaving asks something to remain.

2

When I allow a sea a shape, it too
goes loveless. The slicked black leg

of an egret out-bends the body. When I
loved you, it was baby's-ear small: inside,

impossible empire. Even still. It permitted
flowering. Her body clotting

against mine. Waves folding over
the siltplane for their distant weather.

                              To the left, not far,
a gravel run of river overspills.

A sandpiper creases the water
with its beak.   Nothing tears

3

like boyhood. Even a wave
hates the headland that bears it. What change

is unremarkable. Like the end of love, lighting
there in the doorway leaving so much space,

devastating brilliance.

                    Stones standing themselves
for salt, white astonishment of barnacle
on a crab's brick back.   I've known to come apart

like this: hands standing themselves
from the heart, baring saltlines to the sun.

                    An estuary of only afternoon.
This closed house
holds too little air. An emptied sound swells

against the ear. Whatever might have been said
leaves room, invertebrate, loose in their fine fabrics.

Insistence of recovering tide redistributes
what wealth remains, sediment letting go
its hard-won histories.   It smooths,

again, blown brittlely singular.

4

Even when the door closes behind you –
siltplane palm loosing its lines –
the edges are slit with sunlight.

Not enough to name, but enough to see by.

TO BE REDACTED SHOULD IT
BECOME NECESSARY

Winter again and, though it's early days yet, the sky and I
can sense its restraint. An old redactor's leaving work, stops

in the shop on the corner to grab bread, wine, whatever
is necessary. Milk, maybe – no need to reach for that one all

the way in back, everything will be drunk tonight – the last
of the autumn asters in a pail by the window. Take

only the things that are given. I could have loved you more,
I think. All those evenings, I held you as if I could hold you

together, like syntax. Your hair spilling loose. Past the bare
hotel kitchen, the dusk going soft what with all the gnawing

of dormice in the woodwork, the fallen thistleseed sprouting
in the grass. Birdhouse empty and above. Even unkept, time

keeps us, years, souvenirs, scraps brought back from some
well-planned holiday. Provence. Everything has a limit,

you used to say, the glimmer of city lights failing far below
against the dark. I think of wisdom, now, not so much

as knowing or experience or regret. I could have loved you
through all hours, slipped ourselves loose from them, from

numbering, from needing, and the poem might've ended here.
But I'm told the town's only editor slipped out early tonight

to buy asters, maybe because he knows there's really no use
staying to the end. Or maybe because someone's waiting

at home, and it's been a long time since he's done something
nice for her, something small and more than necessary.

ONLY TIME

... no more,
  These helpless hands.

Virgil, *Georgics* (Eurydice speaking to Orpheus)

Maybe there are enough words. That,
On a night so like tonight, the snow sifting
Fine as sand between the cedars needs

Nothing seems to me an awful lot like proof.
That this line and the firebreak I often walk
Behind the tenements should eventually fold

Back, leaving whole empires unprinted, wild
With fox and winter. That each sentence
Should end in bequest, like small, felt boxes

Each second clicking open. That I can still
Touch, reach out from here where the dark
Begins to wear thin on the dawn. That you

Might, for just a moment, look back. Quiet
Now, like time, you have so much to tell.

§

One thing, one thing, one thing:

But here we are, here where the page ends, hidebound,
hand-held and welled with sleep. Morning. Little left

to say, to sing, to let cling, words like late leaves, like
children. Always, eventually, a last time; all fathers

someday set their daughters on their feet and never
pick them up again. They flock your skin, nevers, slip

like weather off the wing, like the pale after touch gives up
to colour. What is there to do, then, but keep

touching? It's not too much to ask. To leave just one
choice unmade, still warm, a last page unread, a wild

wish wild and unwaited for, one small promise kept
back. Last night's rain is pearling the spruce, the timothy.

But don't wake. Not just yet. I'll glaze our will-not-bes
in lake-long syllables until they're smooth and semi-

precious. I'll set stones along your body. And when
you wake, leave lightly. When you leave, come back.

The introductory note is based on information that is becoming all too familiar in the Treaty 6, 7, and 8 land we now call Alberta, Canada, where wildfires more and more frequently lay waste to great swathes of forest and prairies despite the efforts of conservationists, forestry workers, and wildfire crews to control them. The term "swailing" rarely appears in dictionaries despite being common in some forestry communities. It seems to have origins in Devon, where "to swale" is a dialectal term meaning "to burn" or "to crumple"; it might be related to the term "swelter," which has Germanic origins meaning "to perish."

The epigraphs that accompany section breaks are drawn from (in order): Ludwig Wittgenstein, *Zettel*, translated by G.E.M. Anscombe (Berkeley: University of California Press, 1967); James 3:6; Paul Celan, "Tenebrae," in *Poems of Paul Celan*, translated by Michael Hamburger (New York: Persea Books, 2002/Manchester: Carcanet Press, 1995); Herakleitos of Ephesos, "Fragment 90," in John Burnet, *Early Greek Philosophy*, 3rd ed. (London: Adam and Charles Black, 1920); Lucie Brock-Broido, "A Meadow," in *Stay, Illusion* (New York: Knopf, 2013).

Excerpt from Paul Celan, "Tenebrae," translated
by Michael Hamburger, from *Poems of Paul Celan*
© Michael Hamburger 1972, 1980, 1988, 1995. Reprinted
with the permission of the publishers, Persea Books, Inc
(New York). All rights reserved. And with kind permission
of Carcanet Press, Manchester, UK.

The epigraph of "Spooky Action at a Distance" is my own
invention based on the account related by John Bell in
Speakable and Unspeakable in Quantum Mechanics
(Cambridge: Cambridge University Press, 1987).

"Taxidermy in a House on Fire" is for Tim.

The epigraph of "Shrift" is taken from the first printed
book dedicated entirely to criminal law, William
Staunford's *Les Plees del Coron* (London: Totell, 1557).

"Alta, Leaving" and "Poem, Despite Everything" are both
for Lucie.

"Missive" is for John.

"White Lies" was composed as a loose response to Robert
Rauschenberg's "White Paintings."

"I Was a Dream My Body Had" is for Max, always.

In "The Call," the reference to the *Tao Te Ching* is
deliberately incorrect. It should be that the emptiness of a
bowl or vase is its use (depending upon translation).

"Kwashiorkor" is the term for a severe protein deficiency that causes, among other things, a bloating of the stomach, most often seen in famished children.

The epigraph of "Imaginaria" is from William Shakespeare's *The Tempest*, II.ii.155.

The rough-sketch sonnet shapes of the poems in "Field Studies" take inspiration both from J.M. Turner's series of unfinished "Vignette Studies," a series of preparatory watercolour sketches for his illustrations for 1837 edition of Thomas Campbell's *Poetical Works*, and the techniques of classical Chinese painting. They are in memory of to M.F.

The title, "Call the Wolf a Wolf," was obliquely inspired by Kaveh Akbar's book *Calling a Wolf a Wolf* (New York: Penguin, 2017).

The epigraph of "Not an Elegy" is from Jack Spicer's letters in *After Lorca* (San Francisco: White Rabbit Press, 1957).

"Still Life with Approaching Crow" is after Richie Hoffman.

"Fire, Catching" is for my family, forever.

"The Opposite of Poetry" is for Jackie.

The epigraph of "Augury" is from Andrew Joron's *The Cry at Zero: Selected Prose* (Denver: Counterpath Press, 2007).

The epigraph of "Only Time" is from Virgil's *Georgics* Book IV (the story of Orpheus and Eurydice) from *The Poems of Virgil*, translated by James Rhoades (Oxford: Oxford University Press, 1921).

"Never Say Never Say Never" is for you, whoever you are.

ACKNOWLEDGMENTS

I am enduringly grateful to the editors, staff, judges, and readers for the magazines, journals, anthologies, and prizes who gave homes to the poems from this collection, often in earlier versions. These include: *The Adroit Journal, American Literary Review, Berfrois, Best New Poets* 2016, 2018, 2019, and 2021, *Best New British and Irish Poets* 2019–21, *Boston Review*, Brookes Poetry Centre "Poem of the Week," the Causley Trust Poetry Prize, *Cider Press Review, The Cincinnati Review, Copper Nickel, Contemporary Verse 2, The Dark Horse, Diagram, The Fiddlehead, Harvard Review* Online, *Horesethief, Interpret, The Iowa Review, The London Magazine,* the McLellan Poetry Competition, *Narrative, Narrative* "Poem of the Week," the National Poetry Competition/the Poetry Society (UK), *New Writing Scotland, Oxford Poetry,* the Plough Prize, *Poetry International, The Poetry Review, Poets.org* (Academy of American Poets), the RBC Bronwen Wallace Award, *Sepia Journal, Sugared Water, West Branch*, and the Wigtown Poetry Competition. Thank you, as well, to the editors and editorial teams at Oxford Brookes Poetry Center/ignitionpress and Clutag Press for all your work in honing and promoting the poems from this collection that appear in the chapbooks *Glean* (2018) and *Field Studies* (2019).

Thank you to everyone at the Scottish Book Trust/ Scottish New Writers Awards and Moniack Mhor for providing funding, time, mentorship, and space to write several of the poems in this collection, and I am especially grateful to the family of Callan Gordon for sponsoring

the Callan Gordon Award. Thank you, also, to Carolyn
Smart, to the jury, to RBC, to everyone at the Writers'
Trust of Canada, and to the memory of Bronwen Wallace
for creating and awarding the RBC Bronwen Wallace
Award, which allowed this collection to come into being.
And to Allan Hepburn and the incredible editorial,
marketing, and design teams at McGill-Queens University
Press: thank you for trusting in this work, for giving it
your care, your time, and this stunning form.

This book, like all books, is an inheritance of many
years, many hands, and many words. Far too many to
ever hope to thank and, at any rate, too much is owed.
Nevertheless, I would like to acknowledge, with these thin
marks on the page, the friends, mentors, peers, colleagues,
and students in Canada, the United States, and the United
Kingdom who have both directly and indirectly shaped,
supported, and spurred on both me and this work. I want
to make special mention of my teachers and friends Bert
Almon, Timothy Donnelly, Dorothea Lasky, Alan Gilbert,
Joseph Fasano, David Hinton, Alyson Waters, Alan
Ziegler, Jennifer Franklin, Les Robinson, Niall Munro,
Jackie McGlone, Melissa Lee-Houghton, Anthony Vahni
Capildeo, John Burnside, Don Paterson, and Rosa
Campbell. And, though they could only see the first
inklings of this book, thank you, with all my heart, to
Richard Howard, Max Ritvo, Derek Walcott, and Lucie
Brock-Broido.

Finally, to my parents and brother, engineers and
statisticians who gave me all my first words, who have
supported and encouraged this strange poetic endeavour
beyond what I could ever have asked for, hoped, or
imagined: though you keep insisting to me that poetry
isn't really for you, know that this book, at least, very

much is. And to my partner, my first reader, Isla: you have put up with me, collaborated with me, shaped me to the core, and bring me every day more joy than I could ever put into words. I am so sorry than I have not yet written you that love poem. As someone famous once wrote, "silence is the perfectest herald of joy" ...